VENICE TRAVEL GUIDE

2023

The Ultimate Pocket Guide to Navigating the Charming Canals, Discovering the Art and Culture, and Experiencing the City's Rich History. Everything you Need to Know Before Plan a Trip to Venice

STUART HARTLEY

3

TABLE OF CONTENTS

INTRODUCTION

One of the most stunning cities in the world is Venice, which is situated on an archipelago of 118 islands in a small lagoon connected to over 150 canals. The provincial capital of Venetia is Venice. Due to the 150 canals that function as roads and the more than 400 bridges that connect them, Venice is sometimes referred to as The City of Bridges.

Rialto Bridge is, in fact, the heart of Venice, second only to Piazza San Marco. The Grand Canal Bridge was constructed so that people could cross it, and the 7.5m arch was primarily created to make it easier for maritime vessels to pass. The bridge may be reached with ease. Follow the sign boards if you're walking or using the train.

Venice, with its charming alleyways, waterways, and way of life, is a destination unlike any other. The Grand Canal, a body of water about two miles long, is beautiful. Don't overlook the magnificent historic palaces that the Venetian merchants formerly held.

Additional locations include the Venice Waterfront, the Venetian Ghetto, the Islands of the Lagoon, and numerous other locations. The charming City of Italy, Venice, has countless places to visit.

If you're a traveler who enjoys city exploration and has plenty of time, you must take a walking tour through Venice's narrow streets. First and foremost, you need a very detailed map with instructions and markers that are easy to follow. Second, you should put on cozy shoes. Finally, and perhaps most importantly, you must have very strong feet.

The first settlements in Venice were made in the fifth century when inhabitants from the mainland fled there to avoid the invasions that followed the fall of the Roman Empire. As they struggled to live, these little plots of land surrounded by water gradually began to resemble modern towns. It of a kind location that became the only one of its kind in the entire world.

Venice has a significant cultural presence thanks to its rich cultural past, which includes performing arts, theatre, music, and paintings. The famed Venice cultural Carnival, the major attraction of this Carnival, is the City of Venice's most entertaining characteristic. The Carnival is a fantastic conglomeration of masked parades and festivities.

With 1.6 million residents, Venice is the most beautiful City in Northern Italy, and industry and tourism are big in Venice. This amazing city is charming by the lovely canals, top-notch architectural structures, historical and cultural attractions, and the abundance of restaurants, cafes, pubs, clubs, discos, operas, superb shopping areas, and unbeatable nightlife.

Venice is exceptional, and for a good reason. The list of attractions in Venice is enormous and includes canals, gondolas, imposing structures and churches, galleries packed with precious pieces of art, festivals, delicious food, and fine wine.

Venice is one of the birthplaces of Renaissance civilization. You may walk around this attractive city because it is also recognized as the only pedestrian city in the world. Use cabs and waterbuses to get to different parts of this magnificent city if you don't prefer to walk there.

You'll probably think that you've arrived in the most unusual city you've ever visited when you visit Venice. You will have an unforgettable experience because of the combination of history, culture, and distinctive architecture.

Venice is one of the top travel destinations not just in Italy but around the world. Many couples, honeymooners, and families travel to this lovely location, which features narrow, traffic-free streets winding around canals.

Its sanctuary-like location on a lagoon and near-complete preservation of its historical integrity from roughly 600 years ago adds to its allure. Venetian attractions include stunning churches and palaces, bustling squares, and renowned retail areas.

Venice is shielded from the Adriatic Sea northeast of Italy's country by a section of land known as the Lido. Given its proximity to the water, Venice generally experiences mild weather; however, it does rain frequently.

The city was established in 568 by Lombard invaders who came into Italy from the north. The city was regarded as a Byzantine Empire subject; nonetheless, it eventually attained independence and became a city-state. Venice would develop into a significant maritime power and the hub of the Renaissance and the trade in spices.

Venice holds a unique role in human history. Since Rome, it has been the first illustrious Republic. Il Doge, its chosen ruler of the state, had an insatiable thirst for wealth accumulation and excessive décor spending. At its height, it controlled nearly all the European trade with the Orient and possessed the most potent navy in history.

Venice's collapse caused it to become associated with decadence, a city-state dependent on sex, gambling, and intrigue. Even while it wasn't always gorgeous, it was always fashionable. These days, the Venetian influence may be seen and felt on the dirtiest campus. Its inhabitants continue to be genuinely autonomous people in their hearts.

Napoleon disbanded this old Republic in 1797, ceded their City to Austria in 1815, and incorporated them into the new Kingdom of Italy in 1866. However, Venice's mentality is still purely Venetian, and the locals dislike meddling from the mainland and speaking their dialect of Italian.

The first female gondolier in Venice recently began working for a hotel. The other ferociously chauvinistic gondoliers were outraged, not because she was a woman but because she wasn't a native Venetian.

Almost any time of year is a terrific time to visit the city, although the spring is when Venice is the busiest. You might have trouble finding lodging during the holiday season. Except if you enjoy extremely hot weather and crowded places, summer is a bad time to travel.

There are many attractions in the distinctive City of Venice. Take a traditional boat to appreciate the charming and beautiful waterways; don't skip it. I would advise you to travel in the spring and autumn, and if you can go around Christmas or the well-known Carnival in February, all the better.

Before leaving, check the local weather forecast and pack accordingly. The winters are cool, whereas the summers are hot and muggy. If you travel in the summer, you should usually bring a lightweight jacket or sweater for the evenings.

It would help if you took your time because Venice has a lot to see, and you will be mesmerized by the maze of tunnels and waterways. Visit the Ca' d'Oro, a gallery with great examples of

Gothic art from the 15th century, including works by the painter Titian, if interested.

Ironically, there aren't many suitable swimming spots in Venice. You should visit the Isola di Sant'Elena if you want to run. Regarding rowing, a city with many canals offers more opportunities than you might think.

Venice has much more to offer the traveler than a single trip can cover. Before you see everything there is to see, you might easily visit ten times, and it would take much longer to figure out how to go from one location to another on foot. Venice is a maze, but it's a maze full of incredible gems.

Fortunately, some necessities can be taken care of in a single day. The Ducal Palace, Piazza San Marco, the Basilica, the Campanile, the view of San Giorgio across the Basin of San Marco, and a visit to Caffe Florian are all nearby. Following a path, deciding to see everything in one location, traveling between islands in the lagoon via the public transportation system, or visiting churches, palazzi, scuole, and museums on a personal list are all fun options. Venice will tempt you with delectable options at all times of the day, whether you want to snack, sip something, or enjoy a substantial meal like the Venetians.

The good things in life are valued in this metropolis. Simple guidelines will make this part of your visit easier for you to enjoy.

Steer clear of eateries where the server invites you in. Avoid dining or drinking anyplace near the main shopping streets (the Mercerie), and be aware that you will be paying for the view if you prefer to eat somewhere prettier.

Nevertheless, you'll discover that some viewpoints are worth the extra money. Coffee in Piazza San Marco is a must at least once, and the view along the inflated Riva del Vin is worth the premium. The storied Harry's Bar is small and pricey, but it possesses a charm that can be found in only a few places, making it exceptional. Shopping often follows the same principle. Price decreases with distance from major roads, but you might wish to get a carnival mask from a vendor on the Riva just for the experience.

Those interested in culture, specific architecture, and other types of physical art will find that vacations to Venice have a lot to offer but make an effort to do it in style. It's worth getting personal attention, especially after flying so far. Nothing beats having your guide, boat, car, and business class flights to make a vacation the luxurious and indulgent experience it deserves. Make sure to travel to Northern Italy, Lake Como, and Lake Maggiore because they provide the more affordable luxury items commonly missed during a trip to Venice.

CHAPTER 1: THE HISTORICAL PLACES

Given the variety of attractions available, it is understandable why Venice is one of the most visited towns in Italy. The world's largest collection of architectural works is found in Venice.

Venice's charming and magical city has many historical places to explore. It is hardly surprising that so many tourists are traveling to this region. Many of them have already visited Venice once, and it has managed to captivate their attention. You may find various interesting, distinctive, and one-of-a-kind locations in Venice. Don't skip them when you visit this location, so your stay will be more than satisfying.

When visiting this wonderful city, be sure to check out these attractions.

The Piazza San Marco, where St. Mark's Cathedral is situated, is the town's most popular tourist destination. You can tour the cathedral and even (with some effort) climb the towers to obtain a bird's-eye view of the square. According to legend, St. Mark, the author of the Gospel according to St. Mark, is buried in the cathedral.

Burano island is ideal for strolling along and seeing the vividly colored buildings because it's typically quieter and has fewer tourists.

Six primary areas comprise central Venice: Cannaregio, Castello, Dorsoduro, Santa Croce, San Polo, and San Marco. Each is brimming with unique local appeal. San Marco Plaza, one of the most well-known city attractions, is the sole public square in Venice and has a rich history thanks to the presence of the Doge's Palace and the Basilica San Marco adjacent. The city's most historic district, Castello, is well-known for its Arsenale shipyard.

Santa Lucia Railway Station, which connects Venice to the Italian mainland, is located in Cannaregio on the northern side of the city. The San Polo sector, the smallest part of the city, has a lot of local restaurants and lodging options. The district of Dorsoduro, which includes the noteworthy Dogana da Mar from the 17th century, is located on the southern shore of Venice.

The city's six sestiere are home to churches and palaces of the Gothic, Renaissance, and Baroque architectural eras—the three most striking European architectural movements.

One of the nicest churches in Venice is the Basilica di Santa Maria Gloriosa dei Frari. It is the most notable location among the churches in Venice and is known locally as "Frari." It has Byzantine architecture, with stunning gold mosaics to behold.

Venice's center of power was this ancient castle for more than seven centuries. Due to its lengthy history, it is worthwhile to sign up for a guided tour so that you may learn about the occurrences and tales, such as conspiracies, severe storms, and prisoners. The gothic square's beautiful architecture is combined with an eerie atmosphere from when it served as a courtroom for executions. You may take in the abundance of fountains, statues, and artwork here. You can explore the rooms maintained with medieval items and many interesting stories. You might spend hours exploring the halls because each room has a special, intriguing story to tell.

The renowned Renaissance architect Palladio created a well-known Venetian landmark, the San Giorgio Maggiore church. Several of Tintoretto's paintings, including "The Last Supper," can be found inside.

A guided tour of the Doge's Palace leads you to the area where the government would have operated. There is a jail for Casanova on the property, and the magnificent 500-year-old roof structure is well worth seeing.

The bell tower at Saint Mark is a 1912 structure that is an exact duplicate of the one that fell in 1902. You may get a magnificent view of Venice and the lagoon from the top of the tower.

Canine Palace (Palazzo Ducale). The Venetian ruler's official Palace was this magnificent specimen of Gothic design. It has a thousand years of history, and you may see the priceless works of Veronese, Tintoretto, and Tiziano. Find the area of the Palace where the city's government operated. The roof has the most amazing 500-year-old construction. Not to mention the time Casanova spent in jail before his release.

Tintoretto created Scuola Grande di San Rocco guild house, a masterwork and the pinnacle of Manuelist painting. Mirrors in the ceiling provide a close-up view of the work of art.

Zattere, the Giudecca canal offers a leisurely, sunny stroll insulated from chilly breezes from the north throughout the winter. Across the Canal from San Trovaso, in a Venetian shipyard, you can also watch how a gondola is constructed.

Above all, let the tears roll down your cheeks as you stand in awe of Tintoretto's "Paradise," one of the largest paintings in all of Christendom. It's one of the seven wonders of the world, in my opinion.

The Squero de San Trovaso, one of the very few remaining boatyards in Venice, a significant city that was once one of the largest maritime capitals in Europe, is another tourist destination that is less well known. Here, you may observe gondolas being constructed and repaired.

Although most of them have been turned into hotels, Venice is known for its palaces, so try booking a room there if you can. Although several have been shrunk to accommodate more visitors, most rooms are enormous and have stunning architecture.

Visit the surrounding territory of Veneto, the region's capital city, another item you must do while in Venice. Even if you don't have time to see Verona, the setting of Romeo and Juliet, you should still go to Vicenza.

Vicenza, the birthplace of Palladio, possibly the most influential architect of all time, should not be missed by visitors to Venice. The Rotunda in the town is a typical Palladio structure, and the area is also a UNESCO World Heritage Site. This charming town has numerous Palladio structures, including the Teatro Olimpico, Europe's oldest indoor theatre.

In addition to the Shakespeare connections (The Two Gentlemen of Verona and Romeo and Juliet), Verona is home to the Arena, a beautifully preserved Roman amphitheater. Currently, outdoor concerts are held here. Another ancient Roman city close by is Padua if you enjoy Roman ruins. Italy having Roman cities shouldn't come as a surprise, right?

CHURCH

Saints John and Paul. Many Doges' tombs are in a stunning Dominican chapel with exquisite murals.

Saint Mary Gloriosa of the Friars. A sizable church where you can admire the stunning art and monuments.

Saint Mary of the Miracles. A church with an elegant exterior made of marble facings and a simple design.

The Cannaregio neighborhood is home to the Jewish Ghetto. Since 1152, there has been a Jewish community in Venice, with about 1300 persons. In 1298 it was banned for Jews to stay in Venice; therefore, they moved to Mestre and the adjacent districts but remained given admission to the city for their business activities. Over the years, their ban on stay in Venice was revoked by a proclamation of the "Maggior Consiglio" in 1516; it was decreed that the Jews had to settle in the neighborhood of Cannaregio named Getto. The name Getto comes from the foundries, which produced and provided Arsenal with firearms.

The term "Ghetto" shifted from "Getto" to "Ghetto" to denote the urban regions of European towns where the Jewish community was compelled to live. The Jewish community is still quite active in Venice's Ghetto and abroad. Additionally, five synagogues are located here. Visiting on Saturdays (the Jewish Sabbath) will find all businesses closed.

The sheer number of these structures makes Venice even more impressive. Churches are everywhere, and palaces are pressed up against one another. But Venice is also a city of squares (campI); thus, the finest places to view buildings are in a succession of lush outdoor "rooms" that appear one after the other. Only the city's main thoroughfare, the Canal Grande, is particularly long in Venice, yet even snakes around corners to provide fresh views.

The canals of Venice divide the city into numerous manageable sections, and they transform what might otherwise be a gloomy, tight street into a brilliant border along which gondolas full of tourists with cameras float.

THE GRAND CANAL

Venice contains more than 150 canals and 409 bridges. The Grand Canal is the primary waterway, with gondoliers serenading tourists and locals as they go quickly on evaporators (water buses). The Grand Canal, bordered by more than 170 antique palazzos, provides a window into this lively city's daily life.

The Rialto Bridge, the Ponte Degli Scalzi, the Ponte dell'Accademia, and the Ponte della Constrituzione are the four bridges that cross the Grand Canal.

The Grand Canal is crossed by the oldest and most renowned Venetian bridge, the Ponte di Rialto, constructed in the 16th century using 12,000 wooden posts. Due to its close ties to market activity, it was given the moniker "Ponte di Rialto." Antonio del Ponte constructed the current bridge in 1591, much like the earlier wooden bridge. The bridge includes two inclined ramps where stores have been built and a central portico.

There are stores and flea markets along this arching bridge. **Rialto bridge** is regarded as one of Venice's most illustrious bridges and is well-liked by locals and visitors. You must see this.

Rialto Market and Rialto Bridge locations draw many tourists. There are several small stores and eateries in the East, and the Rialto farmers' market is located west. The bridge has a more than 800-year history and is one of the most famous symbols of Venice. A wooden bridge that collapsed in 1524 was replaced by the current building, which was finished in 1591.

One of the Grand Canal's three bridges is **the Ponte degli Scalzi (Bridge of the Barefoot)**. It was built in 1934 to replace an Austrian iron bridge and was designed by Eugenio Miozzi.

The Ponte dell Accademia, also known as the Academy Bridge, spans the Grand Canal at the Galleria dell Accademia, hence its name. Although it is not a brand-new bridge, its high arch design and wooden structure make it attractive.

The Scalzi Bridge will be the first bridge you cross after getting off the train at Santa Lucia Station in Venice. The Scalzi Bridge, which connects the Santa Croce and Cannaregio areas, was built in 1934 and is named for the nearby Chiesa degli Scalzi, also known as the "church of the barefoot monks."

The Santiago Calatrava-designed bridge was the last to be built in the city (2008). This fourth bridge connects the Santa Lucia train station and Piazzale Roma's parking lot over the Grand Canal.

The Grand Canal's Ca' D'Oro (House of Gold) is a stunning palazzo and a superb illustration of gothic design. A lovely collection of sculptures, tapestries, and paintings may be seen at the Palazzo.

Visiting the Grand Canal while admiring the palaces, sidewalk cafes, and other interesting sights makes Venice well-liked.

Santa Maria della Salute, a Venetian landmark and exquisite Baroque church, stands guard at the Grand Canal's entrance. Paintings by Titian and Tintoretto's Marriage at Cana can be found in the sacristy.

ST. MARK'S SQUARE

Who could ever forget the Piazza San Marco or St. Mark's Square? This is because it is the most well-known location in Venice, which has been regarded as the city's focal point or heart. Since the 19th century, you may discover the significant offices as well as the location of the Archbishop here. Also conducted here are numerous festivals.

In the 12th century, the Columns of San Marco and San Teodoro were placed in Piazzetta after being transported from Constantinople. On top of one column is a statue of San Teodoro, while on the other is a bronze-winged lion that is regarded as a symbol of Venice.

The Piazza San Marco, often known as St. Mark's Square, is Venice's most alluring tourist destination. It is a very alluring location. The finest portion of the square is where you will discover flocks and flocks of pigeons on the floor.

There are roadside eateries there. If you want to feed the pigeons, there are also packets of corn available in the square. There are always a lot of visitors here. The location is accessible throughout the year, but the primary attractions in the plaza have set hours of operation. It would help if you visited the square according to the schedule to see those locations.

Napoleon even went so far as to refer to St Mark's Square as "the drawing room of Europe" since it is one of the most well-known landmarks in Venice and an excellent area to relax and observe people walking by. Even the busiest day of sightseeing is made romantic with a glass of wine at dusk at one of the square's cafes with live music.

St. Mark's Square is dominated by the domes and spires of the Basilica di San Marco, whose beautifully carved gold and marble exterior is one of the most well-known sites in the area. The interior of this 11th-century structure is decorated with golden mosaics, and visitors can either take a guided tour of it or view it from the square's imposing bell tower.

The fact that St. Mark's Square is situated on the banks of the Grand Canal and has so many stunning ancient monuments there makes it the true center of Venice. St. Mark's Square has long been a crucial and essential location in Venice, both politically and culturally.

When you travel, you might also notice wooden walkways or scaffolding encircling the plaza, which are not risers for a performance or concert. Since it floods frequently enough, the city decided to build higher pathways so people could cross the square even when it did.

Go there early morning or evening when most tourists are sleeping or somewhere else to get the maximum enjoyment.

ST. MARK'S BASILICA

A "must-see" is Saint Mark's Basilica (Basilica di San Marco), and the 11th century saw a reconstruction of this structure. More than two square kilometers of exquisite mosaics cover the interior, which also houses treasures like the "Pala d'Oro," a masterpiece of Gothic-Byzantine goldsmithing and priceless glasses amphoras, cups, and icons. View St. Mark's Square from the roof by stepping outside.

St. Marks Basilica is one of the more well-known sights, and you will see why after visiting it. The architecture is stunning, with domes and marble pillars on the outside and top-to-bottom mosaic designs inside. The inside of the church's museums can be toured for a modest cost; however, the church tour itself is free.

The world's premier example of Byzantine architecture is St. Mark's Basilica. The church boasts approximately 40,000 gold mosaics covering the walls and ceilings and is decorated with amazing art pieces.

St. Mark's Square, often known as Panetta, is nearby. Here, you may people-watch while relaxing on one of the sidewalk benches. Take a quick elevator up St. Mark's Campanile to see breathtaking views of the Piazza and Basilica.

Pigeons are also increasing at St. Mark's. You can only feed them in specific locations, so pay attention to the signs to prevent getting fined. It's an intriguing fact that only a limited number of merchants are permitted to sell bird sight in Venice, and these permits are passed down the generations. Today, obtaining a license to sell feed would be extremely unlikely unless it was already in the family.

Another well-liked tourist destination, this magnificent structure is steeped in history. Visit the museums for a deeper understanding of how this structure was created.

Don't overlook the magnificent golden altarpiece in St. Mark's Basilica. St. Mark's Basilica, which dominates the square, is at the top of everyone's list, at least in the country of the Rising Sun. I would say to forget it. Although it appears to be a wonderful building from the exterior, the interior is underwhelming. It is quite dark and ominous, and the air is thick with the smell of old incense.

Given that it is rumored to contain St. Mark's remains, along with more than a hundred other holy sites, Mark must have been a giant among men, if you get my drift.

Undoubtedly one of the most well-known sights to view in Venice is the Basilica of San Marco. To avoid boring readers with just another boring story about how this famous church was built, the

Venetians of the ninth century sneaked the body of their beloved St. Mark out of Egypt inside a barrel of swine fat. Thankfully, his remains are now interred in this magnificent gothic chapel. While the interior features magnificent mosaics and holy artifacts, the outside integrates various architectural influences.

This magnificent Byzantine Basilica sits at the eastern extremity of St. Mark's Square. It was constructed to hold St. Mark's relics, which had been transferred from Egypt in the ninth century. Its enormous marble columns, stunning arches, and domes will astound you. Inside, you can admire a variety of ornaments that merchants brought back after traveling the world for so long. While standing in line to enter is undoubtedly worthwhile, you may also make an online reservation for your ticket. However, you might not be allowed in if you don't dress adequately.

THE CLOCK TOWER

The Clock Tower in Venice, also known as the Torre dell'Orologio, is a well-known landmark in Piazza San Marco. It is considered one of the most important symbols of Venice and is one of the few remaining structures from the Republic of Venice. The Clock Tower was built in the late 15th century and had been functioning as a clock tower ever since. It is a two-story structure, with the clock on the upper level and a small museum on the lower level.

The clock is an impressive work of art, with its two bronze figures of the Moors (Mars and Mercury) striking the hours on a bell. The clock face has 24 hours, zodiac signs, and allegorical figures and is considered a masterpiece of Renaissance clockmaking. The clock tower is one of the most visited attractions in Venice and is a popular spot for tourists to take photos.

Visitors can also go inside the Clock Tower to view the clock's inner mechanism and see the small museum, which showcases the history of timekeeping in Venice and the evolution of the Clock Tower. The museum is open to the public and is a great place to learn about the history and culture of Venice.

Clock tower (Torre dell'Orologio) is another old structure that history buffs will appreciate. A tour guide will take you up a winding staircase to the top of the structure, where you will pass the clock's mechanism. At first glance, this may not seem like much fun, but your opinion will likely alter after climbing the steep stairs to the tower's summit. You can pause and examine the clock's mechanism on the way up.

For a special experience, take a guided tour to the top of the tower. As you ascend a flight of steps, you will pass the clock's mechanism.

Roman numerals indicate time on the reconstructed clock tower, and the Zodiacs and the moon phases are also displayed.

THE BRIDGE OF SIGHS

The Bridge of Sighs, also known as the Ponte de Sospiri, is one of Venice's more intriguing and odd locations. The location is distinctive in addition to its unusual name. This is where the interrogation room in the Doge's Palace is connected to the prison cells. The prisoners can look out the window for their final glimpse of Venice City.

The Doges ruled the Venetian state from their residence, the Palazzo Ducale. You can observe every facet of the Doge's existence, from his residence to the venues for deliberations on questions of state and the administration of justice.

The Bridge of Sighs, which spanned the Rio di Palazzo and was built in the 1600s, was given its name by Lord Byron, who pictured the sighs of prisoners taken in their final vista of Venice before being imprisoned. Passing beneath it in a gondola, taking pictures from the neighboring Ponte della Paglia, or getting a closer view while on a tour of the Doge's Palace are all options for tourists.

The white limestone enclosed bridge includes windows with stone bars, and it links the apartments of the Doge's Palace with the former prisons. The term "Bridge of Sighs" refers to the "sighs" made by Venetian Republic captives during their final opportunity to see the city before being brought away to their cells or the executioner.

THE DOGE'S PALACE.

A historical enthusiast must see the Doge's Palace near St. Mark's Basilica. The Doge Palace is one of Venice's most well-known structures.

The structure has used as a courthouse, prison, and residence for the ruling dynasty. Beautiful medieval statues, columns, and arcades are incorporated into its Gothic architecture.

The impressive Palace where the former Doge of the City resided is called the Palazzo Ducale and is situated near St. Mark's Basilica. If you're taking the water taxi from the airport to Venice, you could pass by, but returning to explore on foot should be at the top of your list.

You'll tour the Palace's chancellery, the torture room, and, of course, the infamous Bridge of Sighs, which can only be crossed by entering the building. The cell from which Casanova fled the prison is another reason to go there.

The Doge's Palace is close by. When Venice was a sovereign state, the Venetians referred to their ruler as the Doge (pronounced "dough-jay"). Although it is opulent and suited for a monarch, most visitors prefer the less luxurious lodgings. Due to his numerous opponents, the Doge added a prison to his Palace, which is accessible by the Bridge of Sighs. The prison can be toured alone, but you must stay on the designated paths. The area is like a honeycomb, so while you are completely free to walk whatever you choose, you risk becoming lost.

Look for the red marble arch that the Doge originally used to supervise public executions and announce death sentences in the square below. To see the Palace can easily take three or four hours. Numerous Italy itineraries already include sightseeing, but if you want to travel independently, many of our guests highly recommend the "Secret tour," Itinerari Segreti, which you may buy in Venice. In addition to a guided tour, the ticket grants access to the entire Palace, the prisons, and the Bridge of Sighs.

This trip to Doge's Palace is highly recommended for history buffs and is conveniently located near St. Mark's. As you finish your tour, take a stroll across the renowned Bridge of Sighs to enjoy a breathtaking panorama of the city.

CHAPTERS 2: MUSEUMS AND ART GALLERIES

It is foolish for anyone visiting Italy to skip a visit to one of the country's many art museums. The world's most amazing works of art can be found in Venice, and there is more than enough contemporary art to satisfy everyone's preferences in addition to classical art. If you plan your vacation well, you'll arrive in Venice during one of the big art festivals, which features around 100 artists' works.

Venice is well known for its artists, musicians, and explorers. Famous residents of the city include Marco Polo, Cabot, Titian, Bellini, Vivaldi, and, of course, Casanova. So it seems to sense that Venice has many museums, art galleries, and other cultural institutions.

The Marciano Museum, the Archaeological Museum (Museo Archeologico), the Accademia Gallery, and the Contini Gallery are a few of the city's top art galleries and museums.

Visit any of the city's numerous museums to get a sense of Venice's lengthy and eventful history. The original bronze horses from the cathedral's façade can be found in the Marciano Museum in St. Mark's Square. At the same time, the Accademia Gallery is home to well-known masterpieces by Italian painters like Tintoretto and Bellini.

Burano, an island in the lagoon of Venice, is well known for its historical lace-making business. Couples can discover more about the art at the Burano lace museum and the Museo del Merletto and view various designs. The delicate fabric is used in many stores in Burano and the rest of Venice that sell items ranging from handkerchiefs to wedding gowns.

Among other artistic treasures, the bronze horses of Constantinople that were brought to Venice during the Second Crusade of 1147–1149 are located in the gallery of St. Mark's Church.

Ca Rezzonico is a three-story museum with a wide variety of artwork, carvings, architectural details, and priceless furniture to adorn each space. However, leave your camera at the hotel, as taking photographs is completely forbidden and is severely enforced by personnel.

Ca' Rezzonico, an 18th-century Venetian palace. As it "recreates" the ambiance of the home of Venetian Nobles, it is like going back in time. You may locate a traditional gondola on the ground floor. This boat is around 11 meters long and 600 kilos in weight. The boat can be moved around the huge stretches of water fast by a single boatman using a single oar.

Peggy Guggenheim, an American collector, lived in the Venier dei Leoni Palace for 30 years. It is now a museum with a stunning collection of contemporary art. Kandinsky, Picasso, Pollock, and Magritte are among the represented artists.

The Museum at Palazzo Fortuny Mariano Fortuny converted this huge Gothic Palazzo in Campo San Beneto, once owned by the Pesaro family, into his studio for painting, photography, stage design, and textile design. Fortuny's chambers and structures, together with tapestries and collections, are still in the building. Mariano Fortuny's office is depicted with priceless wall hangings, paintings, and renowned lamps.

One of Venice's best art institutions, the Scuola Grande di San Rocco, houses an extraordinary collection of more than 50 Tintoretto pieces.

If you enjoy Tintoretto's artwork, you can view it at the San Rocco museum. If you go while a concert is scheduled, you can also take in one. Taking photos is not allowed, so leave your camera at the hotel.

Along with Venice, several significant islands, like Murano, known for its glass, are in the lagoon. Don't miss the wonderful glass museum, which features some incredible blown glass creations, or the Byzantine mosaics in the church of Santa Maria

Assunta on the island of Torcello if you want to get the most out of your trip to Venice.

When it was decided that the glass-making business in Venice posed a fire risk to the city in 1291, it was relocated to the Island of Murano. You can travel there using a Vaporetto, boat, or private water taxi. Visit the glass museum, Museo Vetraio, or take in a glassblowing demonstration.

An intriguing collection of globes is on display at the Correr Museum (on San Marco Square), dating back to the 16th century. A significant picture gallery and an archaeological museum with Roman artifacts are also present.

The enormous bronze horses that once stood outside the Basilica of San Marco are preserved in their pristine form in the Marciano Museum. Manuscripts, pieces of ancient mosaics, and some old tapestries are also on show.

Theater La Fenice This theatre has a long history; it burned down in 1996 and was rebuilt the same way in 2003. Visit utilizing the "audio guide" as it will improve your understanding.

Large San Rocco school. Discover some of Tintoretto's most stunning creations. Additionally, it exhibits a beautiful work of Manierist art.

University Gallery. From medieval collection paintings to Renaissance masterpieces, this Academy of Venice is one of the most esteemed in all of Italy for the Venetian School.

Historical Museum. A significant collection of ancient Greek and Roman sculptures may be found here, including some Greek originals from the classical era.

Pesaro Ca': A stunning palace that houses a modern art exhibition concentrating on 19th-century Italian art.

GALLERIE DELL ACCADEMIA

The Accademia Gallery, which houses the finest Venetian paintings in the world from the 18th century to the present, may be worth a visit if you enjoy visiting art museums. The unique thing about this museum is how they have organized the collections they have amassed in chronological order so that visitors can easily see which are the newest additions and which are the oldest. You should include this on your list of "things to do in Venice."

One of the best art collections in Europe is found at the Accademia Gallery. Works by master Venetian artists like Bellini, Titian, Veronese, and Tintoretto cover the walls.

A visit to the Gallerie dell'Accademia must be on every trip to Venice. The "Homo Vitruvianus" by Leonardo da Vinci is one of its many gems. Must I say more? Just picture yourself staring in awe at a sketch created in 1490 by the greatest artist who ever lived as he attempted to elaborate on the Roman builder Vitruvius' thesis that the proportional relationships of the human body match those used in creating geometric objects. You're there to see the original, but it's also arguably one of the most replicated historical drawings. Something to share with the grandkids.

Since the Roman Empire, Venetians have been renowned for their extroverted personalities and incredible confidence. They had ruled this area for many years, and the drama that followed could be the subject of an entire history book. More tales of intrigue, retaliation, and love were played out at the Gallerie dell'Accademia in this former Palace and current renowned art gallery. Again, participating in an English-speaking tour can be incredibly educational and entertaining. The priceless artworks in this location are primarily by well-known Venetian Renaissance painters.

THE PEGGY GUGGENHEIM COLLECTION

The Peggy Guggenheim Collection is an art museum located in Venice, Italy, featuring the personal art collection of American heiress Peggy Guggenheim. The museum is housed in the Palazzo Venier dei Leoni, an 18th-century palace on the Grand Canal in the Dorsoduro neighborhood.

The collection contains works by some of the most important artists of the 20th century, including Pablo Picasso, Salvador Dalí, Marc Chagall, Max Ernst, René Magritte, and many others. It is considered one of the most important collections of modern art in Europe and is particularly noted for its extensive holdings of European and American Surrealist art.

East of the Accademia Bridge is the Palazzo Venier dei Leoni, home to the Peggy Guggenheim Museum. Modern art is available from the Peggy Guggenheim Museum's private collection. Peggy is an American resident who resided there with her husband, the contemporary artist Max Ernst, for over thirty years. A sculpture garden and pieces by Picasso, Kandinsky, Serini, Duchamp, Pollock, Dali, and Mondrian are included in the exhibition.

In addition to its permanent collection, the Peggy Guggenheim Collection also hosts temporary exhibitions and educational programs. The museum is open to the public and attracts hundreds of thousands of visitors annually.

THE FONDAZIONE QUERINI STAMPALIA.

The Fondazione Querini Stampalia is a cultural foundation located in Venice, Italy. It was established in 1869 by the will of Giovanni Querini Stampalia, who donated his Palazzo and art collection to Venice. Today, the foundation operates as a museum, library, and cultural center, showcasing artwork, books, manuscripts, and other cultural artifacts.

The foundation is also known for its beautiful 18th-century palace, which features a mix of Renaissance, Gothic, and Baroque architectural styles and has been beautifully preserved over the centuries. Visitors to the Fondazione Querini Stampalia can explore its exhibitions and collections, attend concerts, lectures, and other cultural events, and enjoy its beautiful gardens and terraces.

CHAPTERS 3: THE CUISINE AND WINE

The best food in the world is Italian. Italians cook for pleasure, not to eat—forget about France and her unending amounts of horsemeat topped with rich sauces. The key concepts are La Dolce Vita, a culinary adventure, and savoring every moment. The Sun on your back and a song in your heart are everything.

The food and wine that may be savored in the city are last but by no means the least. You can't go wrong whether you go to a well-known location like Pane, Vino e San Daniele, or a local vineyard. After dinner and a few glasses of wine, stroll to a nearby gelato shop to let your meal digest. The best gelato in the city is perhaps available at Boutique del Gelato, one of Venice's most well-known eateries.

Additionally, their wines are exquisite, particularly Barolo and Amarone. Although some aesthetic masterpieces exist, Venice has always been more famous for its business than its art. Try shellfish with Prosecco, a dry sparkling wine, if you enjoy dining as the locals. Of course, most visitors also indulge in traditional Italian favorites like cappuccino or espresso and creamy gelato while in this city.

Most visitors to Venice enjoy sampling some of the top Italian wines produced in the city, including Soave, Bardolino, and Valpolicella. In reality, it's ideal to go from Venice once you've seen everything you want to see and switch bases to travel to other northern Italian regions. Visitors are welcome to stop by and sample the local wines and vineyards.

You may anticipate a wide variety of seafood options when dining in Venice. Several eateries serve seafood, and you may need to drive further inland to find more meat-centric restaurants.

Fish is a distinctive native dish from Venice. It offers collections that are difficult to find anywhere in the world, and even if you did find a few, the scents wouldn't be authentically Venetian. A typical Venetian dish is moleche, a concoction made with green variety crabs. Take a seat at any restaurant and indulge your desire to enjoy a fish dish that stands out from the competition.

The most well-known Venetian fishes in every city corner are sardine, goby, and cuttlefish. In addition to its reputation for fish, Venice combines traditional Italian delicacies, and Pizza, pasta, and lasagna are eternally beautiful recipes originating in Italy.

A break at a pub by the water is another option that is also required. You would also have the opportunity to try a magnificent and fantastic bar on water if you strolled close to the water. Enjoy the city's colorful scenes while relaxing and sipping Italian wine with one hand. The Spritz, a popular white wine in the area, and the Ombra, another favorite among locals for breakfast wine.

If you want wonderful, real Italian food outside of the glamour at affordable pricing, go where the Venetians go to drink. Many off-the-beaten-path taverns and eateries serve great, straightforward fare paired with highly drinking-table wine. Asking the front desk clerk at your hotel for a recommendation for a decent restaurant is a bad idea because he will take you to a place run by his brother-in-law and pocket the commission. It is preferable to rely on your sense of adventure.

For those who struggle with language, the issue with "ethnic" restaurants is that English speakers are few and far between. As a result, sneakily observe what the locals are eating when you enter because you won't understand a word on the menu if there is one. Then, when your waiter comes to take your order, point to a table across from you and say, "quello." That ought to do the trick, along with "vino della casa," and don't forget to flail your arms simultaneously. Then take a seat and anticipate your surprise.

When dining in Venice, it is important to consider the cuisine as a genre. Not to be confused with "Italian" food. Again the cost is secondary to quality here. Go for authenticity over pomp. Traditionally you will start cicchetti at a counter of any bacari. These are little hors d'oevres served with a glass of wine at the counters of pubs. This will peak the appetite for an evening of

47

gastronomical delights. Do not plan on a quick meal in Venice. There is no such thing. The evening meal is an event to be savored. Let the sights and smells be your menu. Servers are more than helpful in recommending just the right delights. Don't forget the Prosecco, a sweet bubbling wine that goes with everything.

TRADITIONAL DISHES IN VENICE

Venice, located in the northeastern region of Italy, has a rich culinary tradition influenced by the city's history as a center of trade and commerce. Here are some traditional dishes that are popular in Venice:

Cicchetti: Small bite-sized portions of food served as appetizers or snacks, similar to tapas. Cicchetti can range from seafood dishes like grilled squid or fried fish to meat-based options like cured meats or cheeses.

Risotto alla Veneta: A creamy rice dish cooked with onions, white wine, and chicken or beef broth. It is often flavored with saffron and sometimes includes pieces of meat, such as beef or chicken.

Bigoli: A type of thick spaghetti made from whole wheat flour and duck eggs, served with a sauce made from anchovies and onions.

Sarde in Saor: A dish of sardines marinated in a sweet and sour sauce made from onion, vinegar, sugar, and raisins.

Bacalà Mantecato: A creamy spread made from salt cod typically served on crostini or with boiled potatoes.

Fegato alla Veneziana: Thinly sliced calves liver pan-fried with onions, served over grilled bread.

These are just a few of the many traditional dishes that you can try when visiting Venice. Whether you're in the mood for seafood, meat, or pasta, there is something for everyone in Venice's rich culinary tradition.

WINES IN VENICE

Wine has been an important part of Venetian culture and cuisine for centuries. Venice is the capital of the Veneto region, home to some of Italy's most famous wine-producing areas, including the Valpolicella, Soave, and Prosecco areas. Here are a few of the most popular wines from the Veneto region:

Valpolicella: A red wine made from a blend of Corvina, Rondinella, and Molinara grapes. It ranges from light and fruity to full-bodied and complex, with notes.

Soave: A white wine made from the Garganega grape, known for its crisp, dry, and minerally character.

Prosecco: A sparkling wine made from the Glera grape, known for its light, fruity, and slightly sweet flavor profile. Prosecco is one of the most popular sparkling wines in the world and is widely consumed in Venice and throughout Italy.

In addition to these well-known wines, the Veneto region produces various other wines, including reds like Amarone and Bardolino. When visiting Venice, try some of the local wines to get a taste of the region's rich winemaking heritage.

RECOMMENDED RESTAURANTS.

Many typical Italian cuisines, such as freshly prepared pizzas, pasta, paninis, cheeses, and salads, are available in Venice's many restaurants, cafes, and diners. Fast-food restaurants and bars, among many others, are available for travelers visiting the city. In the city, notably in the San Marco district, or "Piazza San Marco," outdoor dining is very common.

Venetian cuisine is served in some fantastic restaurants in Venice. Their specialties include polenta, risotto, and spaghetti topped with cuttlefish ink sauce. With the services provided, you will never be dissatisfied.

However, diners should be aware that numerous other establishments offer far lower-quality meals at exorbitant costs for every truly outstanding restaurant or trattoria. A good sign that a place should be avoided is if there is/are a waiter(s) outside the establishment soliciting business while holding up menus.

RESTAURANTS

Antico Martini at Campiello della Fenice, S. Marco, 30124. Antico Martini is an upscale restaurant with lovely décor and a romantic ambiance that draws discerning diners looking to experience extraordinary flavors.

San Polo, 1911, Antiche Carampane restaurant. Located in the center of Venice, just a few meters from the Rialto Bridge. It is a restaurant known for serving authentic Venetian food.

restaurant La Caravella, Via XXII Marzo 2398. This historic restaurant near St. Mark's Square is a must-try if you want traditional meals. They also have a wide selection of wines.

In the back alleys of San Polo, Osteria Antico Giardinetto, Calle dei Morti 2253, Santa Croce, provides traditional Venetian fare such as salted fish and seafood risotto.

San Polo, 778 Antico Dolo. a historic seafood restaurant near Rialto Bridge that sources its daily fresh catch from the nearby Rialto Market.

Do Farai at Dorsoduro 3278. A must-try is their pasta and daily fresh razor shellfish.

Trattoria Dai Fioi. Small trattoria serving food made with regional ingredients.

Small eatery Trattoria Borghi, S. Basilio 1526 is located away from the main tourist area. Well regarded for their pasta and other specialties.

Algiubagio Restaurant, Fundamente Nuove, Cannareggio 5039. What more could one want from the ideal evening than an innovative menu and a subtle ambiance?

San Marco 4685, Bistrot de Venise, Calle dei Fabbri, A historical cuisine of Venice, takes diners on a culinary trip through time to the city's traditional flavors and fragrances.

Restaurant Cipriani: Giudecca 10, Hotel Cipriani, 30133 Venice

The Caravella: Calle Larga XXII Marzo, San Marco 2398, Hotel Saturnia e International, 30124 Venice

Do Leoni Restaurant: Riva degli Schiavoni 4171, 30122 Hotel Londra Palace, Venice

Quadri's Gran Caffe' Ristorante: Piazza San Marco 120, Venice, 30124

Grand Canal: San Marco 1325, Calle Vallaresso, Albergo Monaco e Grand Canal, 30124 Venice

Houdini's Bar: San Marco 1323, Calle Vallaresso, 30124 Venice

The Colombo: San Marco 1665, Piscina di Frezzeria, 30124 Venice

Restaurant da Fiore: San Polo 2202, Calle del Scaleter, 30125 Venice

Toscan Fiaschetteria: Cannaregio 5719, Campo San Giovanni Grisostomo, 30131 Venice

Covo, Al: Castello 3968, Campiello della Pescaria, 30122 Venice

Arturo Vini: San Marco 3656, Calle degli Assassini, 30124 Venice

Harry's Dessert: Giudecca 773, Fondamenta San Biagio, 30133 Venice

Contra Pignolo: 30124 Venice, Calle Specchieri, San Marco 451.

Gondolieri Ai: Venice, Italy, 30123 Fondamenta dell'Ospedaletto, Dorsoduro 366

Mario alla Fava, Da: San Marco 5242, Calle Stagneri, 30124 Venice

RESTAURANT BACARO JAZZ IN VENICE

In how many cities can you find restaurants? It isn't easy to estimate, but given that more than 3 million 500,000 tourists visit Venice a year, you can readily see that the restaurant industry in Venice can be very lucrative, therefore, a large market. Originally only serving seafood, Venice restaurants have expanded to offer diverse offerings. From Chinese to Indian to fashionable nouvelle cuisine to Arab and Japanese cuisine, Venice is attempting to mimic a large city where all kinds of food can be found.

Bacaro Jazz is one of the newest and most inventive restaurants in Venice. It also boasts one of the best and most modern open kitchens, ensuring the complete satisfaction of every single patron.

Since it first opened in December 1997, Alfredo, Nicole, and the staff at Bacaro Jazz have made it a must-visit restaurant and attraction in Venice. Over the years, the restaurant has continuously updated its menu and décor. When it first opened, the restaurant resembled a typical Venetian "trattoria," with locals enjoying "ombre" (glasses of house wine) and munching on "cicchetti" (Venetian tapas appetizers).

The Bacaro Jazz menu offers a delicious eclectic variety of local dishes, some of which are Saor and salt cod, Pasta and beans Venetian style with boiled salami, and cuttlefish in black-ink sauce with polenta. It also offers international cuisine, with some of the standout dishes being Carpaccio raw beef with balsamic vinegar, parmesan cheese, and Red chicory-flavored Tagliatelle. Remember to pair your meal with a great bottle of wine; you can select from a Brunello di Montalcino to a delectable Valpolicella for red wine or a crisp Malvasia for white wine;

Customers can sample two of an excellent range of long drinks and cocktails for the price of one at happy hour, which begins at 4 p.m.! The fantastic drink Frabellini, a traditional Bellini with the sweet addition of Fragolino, is available at Bacaro Jazz in Venice. When the Sun sets, chatting patrons fill the bar's high chairs and order drinks like the homemade "Sex & Sax," a Mojito cocktail, and a Coffee Martini. Couples who prefer privacy will be seated since the restaurant opens its doors to the bar at 11 p.m.

The jazz music that permeates the space couldn't be more appropriate for this late-night eatery in Venice; soft lighting, table candles, and wall posters of the greatest jazz masters give Bacaro Jazz a unique and memorable atmosphere; the décor is truly one-of-a-kind; customers' drawings and testimonials adorn the walls; but if you look up the ceiling, you'll see roughly 500 bras hanging! When customers leave a bra at Bacaro Jazz, they are given a fine T-shirt that reads, "I left my bra at Bacaro Jazz, and all I received was this T-shirt." There are several myths about how the "leave you bra" trend was started; if you're lucky, Alfredo will reveal the truth to you.

San Marco Square is only a few minutes away, and as Vaporettos run all night, you can take one to your hotel or hostel if you stay a little further away from this popular Venice restaurant.

The Florian's Bar in St. Mark's Square is a good place to have an Americano coffee with a shot of hot milk if you're looking for additional places to drink where you have to be seen. Avoid looking George Clooney in the eye while watching the world go by.

The next place you should visit is Harry's Bar on the Lido, especially if you like Ernest Hemingway. After that, you're done.

POPULAR BARS AND RESTAURANTS

- Sportivi, Ai
- Volta Al
- Canine Lounge
- Café Zen
- Sottosopra

CHAPTERS 4: ACTIVITIES AND ENTERTAINMENT

Venice offers a variety of activities, so you may go sightseeing, take in a glassblowing demonstration, go trekking, or sit and people-watch at a sidewalk café. No matter what time of year you visit, this city has many intriguing things to see and do. These places are "must-sees," so be sure to put them on your agenda.

Many parks and green areas, including the Royal Gardens (Giardinetti Reali) and the Giardino Giusti, can be found amid the aquatic City of Venice. Many intriguing and charming places worth seeing are close to Venice, including Burano, which is only a short ferry ride away and is well-known for its lace-making.

Lake Garda, located at the foot of the Dolomites Alpine region and just two hours by rail from Venice, offers breathtaking natural scenery and a variety of activities. There are activities for active tourists like kiteboarding and wind-surfing, as well as late-night shopping, good eating, and trendy nightclubs, so there is something to suit every taste.

The historic and stunning Italian "Water City" offers a wealth of sights and activities. But where do you even begin? You can easily and swiftly enter the city center with Venice airport transfers, so you'll be prepared to begin sightseeing.

Numerous important events, including religious festivals, cultural celebrations, and sporting competitions, occur annually in the Venice region. Seasonal carnivals, the Festa di San Marco at the end of April, the Festa Medioevale del Vino Soave Bianco Soave every May, the Vogalonga rowing regatta in May, the Venice International Film Festival at the end of August, as well as the New Year's Eve masses in the City's Catholic churches, are all events not to be missed.

Visitors may find Venice's numerous festivals and events interesting. A holiday known as Liberation Day occurs at the end of April, and near the end of December, the Immaculate Conception Feast is celebrated.

Carnival (Carnevale) is one of the year's most exciting times in Venice. This city-wide celebration is a stunning recreation of 18th-century Venice that must be seen at least once, but February in the City is inevitably busy and expensive. Consider traveling to Venice out of season because it is busier and more expensive during the International Film Festival and the Biennale in the summer.

Several carnival events in Venice highlight the city's cultural heritage; the more well-known ones typically include the Gran

Corteo Storico, Volo dell Angelo, Sfilata delle Maschere, Festa delle Marie, and numerous other festivals.

The two most well-known costumes for the Venice Carnival are Tragicomica and Mascheranda. Princesses from all across Europe visited Venice during the Carnival, and there was no difference between the common people and the nobles because everyone wore masks.

Anywhere you go, you will discover a city that will stay with you, one that has been a tourist destination since the Middle Ages and one of the few that truly justifies the label "unique." Beat the Curiosity and Visit Venice's Unusual Places

The Chiesa di Santa Maria delta Pieta, the Chiesa di San Bartolomeo, and the Chiesa delle Zitelle on Giudecca are the three best places to hear Baroque masterpieces by composers like Vivaldi. Concerts are held at the Scuola Grande di San Teodoro in San Marco and the Scuola Grande di San Giovanni Evangelista in San Polo, where performers dress in 18th-century costumes and masks and offer their unique interpretations of well-known pieces.

The Carnival in Venice" is a well-liked event among locals and visitors if you are fortunate enough to visit at the right time. It typically begins during the last week of December and lasts about ten days, but this can change. The thirteenth century is when this illustrious tradition first began.

The "mask" and the "Carnival" have a past.

Everyone in Venetian society, from generals to enslaved people, donned masks to commemorate winter while protecting themselves from harsh temperatures.

The Latin term Carnevale, which means "farewell to meat," is the source of the English word "carnival." Meaning a farewell celebration for the meat-based foods that Catholic Christians traditionally sacrificed during the weeks of fasting leading up to the blessed Easter.

Although there have been times when the Carnival of Venice has disappointed as a non-event, such as following Napoleon Bonaparte's conquest of Italy and the subsequent Mussolini administration, the Carnival has developed an unstoppable momentum since the 1980s. This celebration is known as "Carnevale di Venezia" by the Venetians.

Performance art enthusiasts were delighted to see the Teatro La Fenice, a jewel of Venice's opera after it had been destroyed by fire in 1996. High-caliber ballet, music, and theatre are also presented at La Fenice.

The Teatro Goldoni, located between the Rialto Bridge and St. Mark's Square, the Teatro Fenice, Teatro Malibran, and Teatro

Italia are all important theatre venues in Venice, and they all have lovely interiors.

Every two years, the exceptional Biennale festival presents some top contemporary performers in music, theatre, visual art, dance, film, and architecture at prestigious locations. The 2005 event will take place from June to October.

NIGHTLIFE IN VENICE

The nightlife in Venice is thriving, lively, and unmatched. Take advantage of the city's vibrant nightlife if you visit Venice for a weekend or a short vacation. Numerous cafes, pubs, nightclubs, discos, operas, and restaurants are available for your enjoyment.

SHOPPING

Venice is a shopper's paradise. Venice offers you a wide range of options, whether seeking fantastic clothing, antiques, furniture, locally created goods, or computer accessories. Venice has several showrooms, retail establishments, malls, and shopping lanes. The main shopping areas in Venice are Piazza San Marco, the Rialto district, the Mercerie, and Calle dei Fabbri.

The city may be dubbed a "shopper's paradise" and offers plenty of real deals because it has stylish boutiques, independent businesses, and lively markets.

The Mercerie, the vicinity of the Calle dei Fabbri, and the San Marco district are the best places to shop in Venice. Regular fish markets are also conducted alongside the Grand Canal and are well-liked by city residents and tourists.

Take a Vaporetto out to Lido island if you have the time. It's an island with more laid-back (and less expensive) shopping and some beaches, and it is only a short boat-bus trip from the main drag (the Grand Canal).

Venice is teeming with little boutiques that give tourists a wide range of purchasing choices. Any of the shops lining the winding streets sell lovely handcrafted items. Also available in the market are numerous carnival masks, hand-printed marbles, and even writing paper with marbled patterns. Here you may also find leather products and well-known Italian designer clothing.

Murano, an island renowned for its vibrant hand-blown glass, is yet another fantastic place to visit. Venetian shops sell Murano glassware, including pieces with distinctive mille-fiori patterns (thousand-flowers). You may see craftspeople at work and sample a wider range of handmade creations in Murano. Many shops sell things made of Murano glass.

Large-scale retailers can send your glass goods to your home; most shopkeepers can arrange this, at least for larger purchases.

Many options are available; "you may shop till you drop." You can get good quality leatherwear, shoes, wallets, and handbags and discover some unusual clothing in the local boutiques. All your brand-name and label items, such as Louis Vuitton, Prada, Gucci, Giorgio Armani, Versace, etc., are available close to Piazza San Marco.

Try Ca' Macana if you want to buy a mask and observe its creation simultaneously. If you can't find a mask that appeals to you in this store, perhaps you didn't want it in the first place. For an amazing variety of handmade masks and costumes, check out Atelier Marega.

When shopping, watch out for imitations and fakes of well-known brands. A few examples include Murano Venetian glassware, for which the Government of Venice protects Murano glassmakers by placing a decal with the trademark "Vetro Murano Artistico" at showrooms and stores that sell genuine Murano glass. The wonderful tiny structures by "Moro" are another small collector's item, and to combat fakes, he writes his identity on the back of each one.

RIALTO MARKETS

For more than a thousand years, the people and chefs of Venice's most prestigious restaurants have relied on the Rialto Markets for food and goods. The Venetians have been aware of the value of sustainable fishing methods for generations, and their rules are still in force today. Fresh seafood and veggies are essential in this region, and most chefs arrive here every morning at the crack of dawn with their ingredients. You can enter this historic market by passing over the charming Rialto Bridge. Along with a wide variety of other curiosities and treasures, you can sample and purchase some of the freshest and most distinctive foods available anywhere in the world. In the city, you must see it!

Explore the Rialto market to uncover sought-after regional specialties local farmers and fishermen offer, or stop by one of the wine bars for a drink.

Every morning, the bustling Rialto Markets are open. There is a selection of food, clothing, and souvenirs. Don't miss the live lobsters and crabs at the fish market, which has been held in this location for 1000 years.

GONDOLAS

The Venetian gondolas, which are as old as the canals, are an integral element of the city's environment. Gondola is one of Venice's most recognizable emblems around the world. This exceedingly old Venetian boat is the product of intricate processes. The average Gondola is 11 meters long and 600 kilos in weight. Given its weight and size, it is incredibly simple for one person to move.

The Gondola is one of the more popular modes of transportation in Venice. You can take Gondola rides and explore any of Venice's smaller canals.

Without thinking of canals and gondolas, one cannot imagine Venice. The city forbids the use of automobiles, and all mobility is by water. Take the Vaporati (water bus) and navigate the Grand Canal like a real Venetian. It will take you beneath the Rialto Bridge and is the ideal approach to take in the stunning palaces that line the Canal.

Of course, when one thinks of a city, they immediately picture a gondola, complete with singing, striped shirt wearing, and the appropriately mustachioed gondolier. It may come as a shock to learn that this type of set-up is now largely a tourist attraction rather than a "real" means for Venetians to get around since it has been at the center of many classic love scenes and is still seen as a particularly romantic activity to partake in as a pair.

A keen-eyed visitor might still catch a glimpse of the occasional Gondola passing by as they make their way from Venice airport to Venice. Still, this mode of transportation is slowly but surely vanishing, having already been replaced by more effective types of vessels in the city's daily life.

Many people cannot understand the labor that goes into each Gondola when riding in one. They come in 280 pieces and are composed of 8 different types of wood. Also, note that the Gondola has a longer length on one side than the other to help balance the gondolier's weight.

A gondola excursion is one of the most well-known and fun things to do in Venice. Every visitor to Venice is required to take a gondola cruise through the canals. But you must be aware of the following when looking for a gondola:

There are two distinct gondola kinds.

Beautiful gondolas with good seats and occasionally with flowers are available and beautifully adorned and maintained. And then some are less beautiful and simpler than others. When renting the first kind of them, the cost is typically higher.

Tours and promenades come in two varieties.

Serenata-infused and non-infused versions. It's a prevalent belief that some "gondoliers" will serenade you while singing a piece of music. However, if you want a tour with Serenata, the price will go up, which is not true. The easiest way to get a tour with serenity is to reserve a tour at the tourism office, where they can educate you about the unique gondola tours.

You have to barter. It takes time to find good pricing.

The cost of taking a gondola tour is generally high. But you need to look around and get price quotes from various "gondoliers." The average cost of a 50-minute gondola tour is 100 euros, and a 30-minute tour is 60 euros. The promenade typically costs 80 EUR for 50 minutes for the simpler ones.

At night, the costs are higher.

The "gondolier" raise their prices as dusk falls. It's recommended to take the tour in the afternoon, before eight o'clock, because the prices are more affordable, even though doing the tour at night can be a great alternative if you're a couple because of the romanticism and all that.

The cost of riding in a shared gondola is reduced.

It can be a wonderful choice to save money on the tour if you don't mind going on it with other people. One Gondola may hold up to 6 passengers!

BOAT RIDES AND INLAND EXCURSIONS.

The boat ride from the airport sets the scene. Marshes and other bodies of water may be seen for a minute before you get your first look at the city, which is nothing short of stunning.

The Campanile, the newest in Venice, dominates the skyline after replacing the previous structure of the same name that collapsed in 1902. It stands erect on the outskirts of St. Mark's Square, where your journey starts.

To reach the Venetian islands, a motor launch journey through the Venetian Lagoon. The Arsenale, St. Elena, and the Church of San Pietro di Castello can all be visited on this particular route. One can also take in the breathtaking sights of the Grand Canal as they travel by St. Mark's Basin.

Another option is to travel to the little island of Murano, which is well known for being a hub for manufacturing glass. A glass factory tour allows visitors to learn about glass objects' production process and make any necessary souvenir purchases.

On San Giorgio Island stands San Giorgio Maggiore, one of Venice's most significant churches. The Last Supper and "The Gathering of Manna," two of Tintoretto's most outstanding creative creations, are housed in this unassuming chapel.

You can also hire a tour guide to stroll some of Venice's winding lanes and crowded piazzas. Imagine yourself exploring the complex labyrinth of secret passageways, all the tiny canals, the magnificent structures, and the elaborate bridges, which all represent the distinct Venetian beauty and charm. The Square of Campo San Polo, one of the larger and older piazzas, was once used for religious events and theatrical plays in antiquity.

Try to avoid skipping the Islands when you are organizing your trip to Venice. The peaceful town of Torcello features an antique church. Burano is a charming maritime village where you can visit the Lace Museum and enjoy the picture-perfect streets with pastel-colored houses. San Geogio is dominated by the San Giorgio Maggiore facade, arguably Palladio's most beautiful work in Venice. The church is filled with treasures.

Murano Island is renowned for its Venetian glass craftsmanship. Murano's nickname, "Murano Colonna," derives from the still-present granite column. The many glassworks is among the attractions associated with glass. Sadly, several top glassblowing factories are not accessible to tourists, though some offer demonstrations. A glass museum is also located in the island's center, in Palazzo Giustinian.

Be wary of con artists who offer you a free boat excursion to see the Murano glassworks. Prices go up too much, leaving you stranded if you don't purchase. Many gift stores attempt to pass off inexpensive Chinese knockoff glass as genuine Murano glass, and government officials in Venice safeguard Murano glass production. So, when visiting showrooms selling genuine Murano glass, seek the "Vetro Murano Artistico" trademark decal.

CHAPTER 5: WALKING ITINERARIES

The majority of Venetians commute by foot, and you presumably will as well. The city has all the turns and bends you would anticipate in an old town. You may occasionally find yourself in the intriguing situation of seeing where you want to go but not being able to figure out how to get there due to the network of canals. In Venice, there is nearly always something interesting to view, so even if you get lost, you'll probably still see a lot of amazing sights.

48-HOUR VENICE TRAVEL GUIDE

You might have time to explore after checking in, provided you haven't spent most of the day trying to find your lodging. The absence of traffic is one of the first things you'll notice. Only Piazzale Roma, the remaining open space close to the train station, is allowed for vehicles. Your journey starts here, along with the bus terminal and open parking lots.

10:00

You might be wondering what motivated the early settlers to create their city afloat on 117 tiny islands in a swampy lagoon as you cross the first of 409 bridges across the 150 canals. The main justification was safety and defense against the raging, non-swimmer Attila the Hun.

However, the natives quickly discovered that the central location was just as crucial for European trade.

Even just strolling through Venice's streets is fun. Byzantine, Renaissance, and luxurious Austro-Hungarian aesthetics are all mixed together in the architecture. Narrow pathways wind around corners to reach secret gardens or lead into ornate courtyards. Some structures have an unsettling lean that can make you feel queasy, and I hope they are still standing in a few minutes as you pass by.

With arrows pointing either to Piazzale Roma, "Ferrovia" (the train station), or toward Piazza San Marco, and frequently in both directions, three primary street signs are most visible. Most tourists can easily reach San Marco because of the wider street lanes, but it is advised to venture off the main path to see Venice truly.

12:00

Turn a few more times, and after a few hours, you will have completely lost and found yourself again, presumably in Piazza San Marco or at the Ferrovia.

The Campanile that towers over you will be the first thing you notice.

On Roman-era foundations, the Campanile was constructed as a lighthouse and watchtower. Over several centuries, it was expanded and added to the point where it completely collapsed in 1902, prompting a massive worldwide effort to reconstruct it brick by brick. The falling bricks entirely broke the logetta base relief at the foot of the tower, which had to be meticulously put back together. The view of the distant islands across the lagoon from the top of the Campanile makes the ascent worthwhile and serves as an excellent navigational tool. Even here, Galileo gave the Doges a telescope demonstration.

The overwhelming amount of pigeons is another conspicuous feature that dominates the square. They frequently surround young children whose parents have generously covered them in bird feed, expecting the birds to carry them away. On a slightly more sombre note, there is a rumor that anyone found kicking the birds will be fined $500 US. Although quite appealing.

Looking south, you'll notice watercraft bobbing about, including the vaporetti, Venice's metro system, transporting employees and tourists from island to island. The pillars supporting the statue of St. Theodore and the winged lion, the City of Venice's symbol, are topped with these watercraft. Then there are the water taxis, delivery boats, police, fire, ambulance boats, and the recognizable black gondolas.

During your walk, you would have seen boats smoothly gliding through the canals between the houses with couples and groups of visitors on board, being driven by striped-shirted guys pulling a long oar and perhaps singing an opera aria.

You'll exit the square's most southern edge by continuing past the Doges Palace and turning left. Another bridge needs to be crossed, yet it can appear busy with tourists as they glance up a canal at another bridge. The Ponte Sospiri, also known as the Bridge of Sighs, is the subject of their curiosity. A covered bridge connects the palace courts with the former prison. Before being hauled off to the "leads," captives might gasp for one last breath of fresh air at the small latticed window.

14:00

Returning to the Rialto Bridge is the next step. There will be a few signs pointing you in this direction, and once more, they might look like they go both ways. Of the three bridges in the world with stores, this one is the oldest.

The Rialto served as the commercial hub of medieval Europe, as traders from the East delivered commodities to affluent Venetian merchants. Usury, or money lending, was also practiced, greatly boosting the city's finances and making Venice incredibly affluent.

After a competition was held to resolve the ongoing issues of flooding and fires that kept destroying the wooden ones, the stone bridge was built in the 1500s.

78

Antonio da Ponte, an architect, won it with ease. Additionally, it needed to be tall enough for vessels traveling to the crusades to pass beneath.

It may be appropriate to board a Vaporetto to travel along the Grand Canal, depending on where you are staying or how tired your feet are. You may travel 40 minutes along the Grand Canal, pass beneath the Rialto, and see the spectacular houses, palaces, and opulent Venetian hotels that line the banks for a fraction of the price of a gondola ride.

19:00

Venetian canals are only used by gondolas and the occasional taxi at night when there is much less noise from the boats going about their daily business. Eating out can be expensive if you don't know where to go. A general rule is that prices decrease the further you are from Piazza San Marco. However, some affordable locations are still nearby in areas like Cannareggio, Dorsoduro, San Polo, and Santa Croce. While some pubs also serve bar snacks and light meals, they focus more on osterias.

Due to the high living expense, many Venetians no longer remain in the city and instead choose to live in Mestre on the mainland. As a result, the nightlife isn't extremely vibrant after hours. You can purchase expensive cocktails in a select jazz bar. The most well-known location in Venice is Harry's Bar in San Marco, where the

Bellini was created. It tastes good to mix champagne with peach juice.

09:00

Getting going early is essential to ensure you get where you're going and, ideally, beat the crowd. There doesn't seem to be a low season in Venice because it is a very popular city all year long, both in the summer and the winter. The weather can occasionally be advantageous because it can keep large crowds at bay and shorten line times. In the winter, flooding is typical.

A long line of people shuffle through the doors, or you quickly enter the Basilica. Due to years of flooding, the floor feels uneven, so be careful where you tread. The bones of St. Mark, the city's patron saint, are located beneath the altar. St. Mark was a replacement patron because the city leaders believed St. Theodore had sufficient clerical authority.

The mosaic depicting the return of St. Mark's body from Alexandria, Egypt, in 828 is located above the door on the left. A chapel was built to hold the remains but burned down in 932. In its stead, a larger basilica was built in 1063. St. Mark's body was misplaced during some restorations, but it was finally recovered and moved to the crypt below the altar.

The Quadriga is positioned on the loggia balcony above the doorway. The four horses you see here are replicas of the real ones kept inside the Galleria, and they were taken during Constantinople's siege. For a nominal charge, you can access the Galleria upstairs, where you can see the original horses and have a fantastic view of the Basilica's interior.

10:00

The Palazzo Ducale was started in the tenth century as the official house of the Doges. These guys were in charge of the entire Venetian republic's administration, legal system, and government.

Paintings, frescoes, and sculptures cover the walls and ceilings of the chambers and passageways. Tintoretto's paradise, one of the biggest oil paintings ever created, stands out in particular. Numerous pieces on display by Tintoretto, Sansovino, and Veronese represent the prosperity traders brought to the city.

You can also cross the Ponte Sospiri to the palace prisons, giving you a chance to imagine how the captives must have felt as they were being led away to be imprisoned. The notorious womanizer Casanova, who was the only one to escape from the State Inquisition's prison for involvement in the "occult" in 1755, was one of the more well-known residents.

14:00

Numerous stores and churches are lining the streets in the San Marco neighborhood, all of which showcase more exquisite works of art, architecture, and quality. Last but not least is the magnificent Chiesa di Santa Maria della Salute, the church across from the square that serves as the Grand Canal's entryway. The people believed the Virgin Mary had shielded them from a plague epidemic; therefore, this church was constructed in her honor during the 17th century.

15:00

You can reach the Dorsoduro Peggy Guggenheim collection by continuing up the Grand Canal. She spent her final 30 years in Palazzo Venier dei Leoni before passing away in 1979. Picasso, Mondrian, Chagall, Ernst, Miro, Magritte, Bacon, and Dali pieces can be found in her collection. More sculptures can be found in the garden, along with Ms. Guggenheim's and her dogs' graves.

10:00

From Fondamente Nove, take the LN line vaporetto for 10 minutes to reach Murano, where glassmakers have been practicing their craft since 1291. Venetian glass was formerly one of the most coveted possessions of the affluent in Europe and is still highly regarded. The glass makers were relocated here by ducal order following a string of fires, and they faced treason charges if they attempted to leave the city—such as the value placed on their expertise in the trade. Watch for signs with the word "fornace," as you can currently observe them in action on their property. Even more, structured, guided tours and demonstrations are available in some locations.

12:00

The 30-minute trip from Murano-Faro to Burano can then be continued. Lace-making has a long history, and it originated in Burano. The lace, an extension of the fishing nets fashioned by the island's women, had a reputation as being of the highest caliber in courts throughout medieval Europe. The island stands out partly because of the vivid colors used to paint the homes.

16:00

The Lido, Venice's magnet for celebrities and movies, is an hour away from Burano. Every year, the Venice Film Festival takes place here, drawing celebrities from all around Europe and, increasingly, beyond Europe. The seashore offers some relief from the bridges even though the stars are not visible. Although the resort is no longer as trendy as it once was, more affluent travelers are nonetheless targeted by the costs. It should take roughly 15 minutes to return to San Marco.

CHAPTER 6: LODGING AND TRANSPORTATION

Venice is unique above all other places globally, and the city comprises a maze of canals, magnificent bridges, cobblestone streets, and bustling squares. On foot or by Vaporetto, a network of boats that serves as the city's primary transportation source, explore this wonderful city's distinctive landmarks.

In Venice, there are more visitors than locals, and there are a variety of lodging alternatives to suit any budget, from luxurious private villas in Italy to modest guesthouses and hotels. The ideal seasons to go are spring and fall when there are fewer tourists around, and you can get great deals on lodging and other amenities. Between October and January, it floods roughly 60 days per year.

A large stretch of sand known as the Lido protects Venice's lagoon from the sea. Families and sun lovers enjoy day trips to the island because of its beautiful beaches.

Public transportation is widely available throughout the city but can get very busy. Many ride the spacious water buses (vaporetti), which are rightfully famous. They are managed by ACTV, which oversees transportation in the city and surrounding lagoon. However, they are not inexpensive; at the time of this writing, a normal single price was about €7. If you intend to travel extensively, you can get special extended passes that will save you money. If you're wondering how locals manage it, the solution is straightforward: as residents, they receive a significantly reduced tariff.

A water taxi is another option. Prices vary greatly, but they're unlikely to be considered "affordable."

The cost per passenger will start to look more appealing if you can arrange to share one of the cabs, which some taxis can accommodate multiple persons in.

However, unless they're planning a trip to one of the lagoon's islands, most visitors prefer to travel on their own two feet. The city's historic district is compact, and the most popular tourist attraction can be reached on foot in no more than 30 minutes.

HOTELS

Leading the pack is the pricey Hotel Cipriani, which is also over there on its island, approximately 15 minutes boat ride away, with no views. Additionally, just the bar tab will cause you to have a heart arrest.

Better positioned is the Hotel Danielle. Even though it's in the wrong part of the city and has a dull ambiance, at least it's in the city.

The historical significance of Venice adds aesthetic appeal to the front of Venetian hotels. Some are even more distinctive hotels for travelers because they were constructed from exquisite historical houses like palaces.

Cipriani Hotel and Palazzo Vendramin. The Hotel Cipriani, a renowned Orient-Express hotel, is located on the point of Giudecca Island and is connected to the Palazzo Vendramin and adjoining Palazzetto by a historic courtyard and floral passageway. From here, guests can enjoy the stunning views of the lagoon and the Doge's Palace. It is well-known for its gorgeous interiors furnished with regional treasures and is steeped in Venetian style.

San Clemente Palace Hotel at di San Clemente 1, San Marco. Set on the 17-acre private island of San Clemente, which dates back to the 12th century and is a pristine refuge on the Venetian lagoon with stunning views of St. Mark's, Giudecca Island, and the Lido. By free shuttle boat, St. Mark's Square may be reached in 12 minutes.

San Marco Bauer Il Palaz Hotel. This five-star luxury hotel is housed in a historic palace from the 18th century. It offers exquisitely designed and equipped rooms with gold-plated mirrors, tapestries, Murano glass chandeliers, and other furnishings. The Grand Canal, Saint Marc basin, and the majority of the town are visible from the balcony or terrace of the majority of rooms.

The Rialto Hotel San Marco; Riva del Ferro / Ponte di Rialto; is at the center of Venice's commercial, artistic, and historical life. Rooms and suites in traditional Venetian architecture. It is at one of the city's most picturesque and suggestive locations, directly across from the Rialto Bridge, overlooking the Grand Canal in a special and ideal location.

Hotel Marconi, Riva del Vin, San Polo. The renowned Rialto Bridge on Venice's Grand Canal is seen from the Marconi. The interior design of the apartments is classic Venetian, and historic marketplaces and authentic Venetian eateries are all around it.

Doge Orseolo and Albergo Cavalletto. San Marco. One of Venice's oldest hotels with a more than seven-century history of catering to distinguished people. The Cavalletto Doge Orseolo has hosted guests, including the Duke of Aosta, Richard Strauss, and Sir Winston Churchill. The hotel has traditional Venetian rooms facing Bacino Orseolo and is just a few meters from St. Mark's Square.

Giorgione Hotel: Cannaregio Ss. Apostoli in Cannaregio, Georgia. The Hotel Giorgione is the perfect choice if you want a beautiful atmosphere in Venice. It is housed in an 18th-century structure with a lovely courtyard and fountain. The Giorgione Hotel, transformed into a deluxe hotel in the early 19th century, has preserved its upscale ambiance with ancient Venetian furniture, Murano glass lights, and luxurious fabrics. The hotel is located in the peaceful yet strategically located Cannaregio neighborhood, about 5 minutes from the Rialto Bridge and 10 minutes from Saint Mark's Square.

Gottardi Ca' , Cannaregio, 2283 - 30121. One of the most upscale boutique hotels in Venice, Ca' Gottardi is a classic Venetian Inn & Guest House with a historic palace adjacent to the Rialto Bridge. Here, traditional art and cutting-edge design come together with remarkable elegance.

Cavalletto Hotel. San Marco, 30124, 1107. All rooms feature traditional Venetian furnishings, and a few have lovely views of the gondolas in the Orseolo Basin.

Residenza Ai Giardini Castello 747-448, Venice 30122, is an establishment that stands out from other accommodations for tourists by having genuine, magnificent apartments.

Ca' dei Dogi at Corte Santa Scolastica in Castello 4242. An old Venetian castle from the fifteenth century with typical features like marble and mosaics, It is close to the Bridge of Sighs and the Palazzo Ducale.

Antiche Hotel Figure. Santa Croce 686. This hotel offers a lovely garden café where you can unwind with a drink after sightseeing and is conveniently situated about 300 meters from Santa Lucia Station. The figure is gazing affectionately at the Grand Canal.

In the center of Venice, at S. Croce 2063, Hotel Al Ponte Mocenigo is easily accessible. Its ten exquisite rooms, which blend classic elegance and contemporary comfort, are spread across two levels of a beautifully renovated property in a quiet area.

Naturally, there are many more accommodations worth mentioning; nevertheless, we cannot include them all.

TRANSPORTATION AVAILABLE FOR GETTING AROUND

The traditional boat in Venice is called a gondola, which used to be the principal mode of transportation. Venice is a very pleasant experience since it is readily walkable and has no cars, making it a particularly pleasant experience. For example, walking from one end to the other takes an hour. Use the vaporetti, sometimes known as water taxis or water buses, to move around swiftly. The canals are lined with vaporetti in great numbers.

Or, you may bring the enchantment of Venice to life by taking a Grand Canal tour in your motorboat. You will discover the history and development of the "Grand Canal," the most significant street in Venice. All boats are outfitted with microphones and speakers so you can easily hear the thorough commentary your guide provides as you travel along on this fascinating tour while sitting comfortably.

But riding a gondola up Venice's Grand Canal and the numerous smaller canals is the most romantic and greatest way to admire the beauty and singularity of this amazing city built on water. Exploring the city's various neighborhoods and taking pleasure in a complete introduction to Venice. The Gondola is perfect since it is tiny enough to travel through the smaller canals. The magnificent palaces, churches, bridges, gardens, and warehouses line the city's waterways.

Gondola rides through the city's waterways are what make Venice famous throughout the world. The Venetian Casino and Hotel in Las Vegas incorporates a significant portion of this particular aspect of Venice. The casino ride is enjoyable, but it is nothing compared to the real deal. This is the ideal location to visit on a special night. While the gondolier performs a passionate song, tour the city. Could things possibly get better?

Speaking of boat trips, take a vaporetto down the Grand Canal if a gondola ride is not your thing, and it is the ideal activity for passing an hour or two while seeing the city.

PUNTING IN VENICE

Unquestionably, one of the most famous ways to explore Venice is by Gondola punting. There is something inherently ageless and beautiful about traveling through this wonderful city's canals and rivers. Although nowadays punting is mostly only done by visitors, it used to be a sign of status in this distinctive Italian city. Consider including a punt ride during your trip to Venice if you intend to go there.

The Background of Venice's Punting

Canals were created relatively early in Venice's history due to the land's lagoon-like characteristics, and the city's being made up of more than 100 tiny islands. Punts were created because using these canals required specialized types of water transportation. Early in the first millennium, gondolas are thought to have been utilized for the first time in Venice.

Gondola transportation was only afforded to the city's affluent residents, and regular citizens didn't typically enjoy punting along the city's canals. Gondola travel has historically been more about spectacle than it has ever been about getting around; it's not exactly the quickest or most effective way to get around Venice. Although gondolas and punting have passed their prime, they play a significant role in every local celebration. As the world's biggest urban area without automobiles, Venice offers visitors a rare chance to experience the peace and joy of punting around its canals.

Today's Punting in Venice

You undoubtedly want to know how much it will cost to experience punting while visiting Venice. There are set fees in place; a 40-minute gondola journey for six persons costs about £70. For around £35 you can extend the excursion by another twenty minutes. These prices are for a straightforward punt through a few canals; longer journeys, such as those with gondoliers who sing love songs, can cost up to £125 for forty minutes.

Despite its hefty cost, a Venetian punt is well worthwhile. The two most well-known bridges in the city—the Rialto and the Accademia—and several Venice hotels are convenient locations to pick up punts. Set aside some extra money when organizing your trip to Venice so that you can take a traditional gondola ride. You might easily scrape the additional cash by reserving inexpensive hotels in Venice. Who knows whether you'll ever have another chance to explore this magnificent city in such a better way?

CONCLUSION

Venice is a treat to pass through, and the city promises its prominence and glory will never weaken the visitors. The view of the city from a bird's eye perspective is captivating since it appears to be a saffron engineering structure on the turquoise waters.

More than 30 million tourists visit Venice annually, or over 60,000 visitors per day. It's simple to get to Venice, and it is quickly possible to purchase airline tickets from everywhere in the world. If today is your day of reckoning, you might be able to snag some last-minute inexpensive airfares. Venice experiences moderate winters and sunny summers, making it a pleasant place to visit.

Driving in Venice is more of an adventure, and walking or using the conduits are the two main ways to move around the city. Venice's strolling has a distinct allure and taste. Strolling along a mid-lash with a water feature on one side and a beautiful Italian design on the other.

In the tidal pond area, waterbuses are the main source of transportation. These waterbuses follow regular routes via the Grand Canal to the city islands. Wandering the Gondola is a must-do activity while you're here if you want to experience the city. The local Venice watercraft, known as a gondola, will ferry you through the city's waters. A 30-minute ride with a maximum entry of 6 people would cost about 80 euros.

The traghetto and water taxis are alternate modes of transportation significantly less expensive than the Gondola. The City on the Mainland features a cable car system and a regular course of transportation for daily driving.

Couples can take the Orient Express into the city if they want to ensure that every aspect of their trip—from selecting the ideal Venice hostels to choosing the best transportation—is romantic. The renowned train travels on several itineraries that stop in Venice, including Venice-Budapest-London and London-Paris-Venice.

The old city core is nearly entirely devoid of automobiles, so why not go in elegance by choosing a gondola ride through congested canals and beneath charming bridges? Although this ancient mode of transportation is pricey, it allows tourists to truly experience the spirit of Venice, especially if the gondolier serenades them while they travel.

Venice deserves praise for its stunning architecture. The city encloses a being in its alluring Gothic architecture. Over 500 years old and yet standing tall with respect and joy are some of the Venetian plans. Piazza San Marco is a priceless location in lovely Venice, and the intersection of the city's three main attractions is this fantastic square.

The main attraction of Venice is the Basilica of San Marco on one side. The congregation is frequently packed with admirers, as well as more people from the general public who came to observe the splendor of this artistic legacy. The city's foremost specialist resides at the Doge's Palace on the other side. This castle was built in the fourteenth century and had a rich style and expression. It adds artistic climaxes from Tintoretto and Titian to the 1000-year history of Italy.

Another creative and dilatory design of the Venetians is the Torre dell'Orologio, a clock tower on one side of San Marco Square. Italy's design is frequently taken into consideration. At every corner of the city, you can find an eye-opener. San Giorgio Maggiore, Santa Maria Della Salute, and Palazzo Ducale are a few other outstanding places that must-see.

It is not necessary to book far in advance because there are always last-minute cheap flights to Venice. Spend a few days off from work and visit this magnificent and unforgettable retreat.

In Venice, taking an extended stroll across the city requires a commitment. The city transforms into something magnificent when you go along the quaint streets. Venice stands apart from other cities of its kind due to the inclusion of wonderful design and scenery. You may shop instead of wandering through the City; Italy is certainly the world's capital for architects.

It is typical to fall in love with the city the moment you arrive, so make sure to factor in a few additional days when arranging travel arrangements to Venice. There is romance in the air daily, and fresh adventures are to be had. Venice should be at the top of your list of places to visit if you only take one trip abroad in your lifetime.

Made in United States
Orlando, FL
06 April 2023

31826818R00054